I SIT HERE THINKUN

by

Tina Chamberlain

MUM AND DAD

My mum and Dad were my best friends
They always made me laugh.
In my younger days
I would sit and laze
By the fire, in an old tin bath.

I remember the old Honey Cart
When we used to have outside loos
You'd hear the tin rattle
As the men came to battle
And clear away all of your doos.

My Mum or Dad would stay with me
If I wanted to go! In the night
Sometimes with a nail, dad would tap on a pail
And blast that would give me a fright.

As the youngest of nine I remember
The hard times as well as the good
When mum didn't bake
She would sit down and make
Clothes and curtains as best as she could.

They were both very hard working and honest
Nothin to them was a chore
All day mum worked steady
And had the tea ready
For dad, when he came in the door.

They both had a great sense of humour
And dad he told jokes like a star
He would take mum for trips
Just to get "fish n chips"
That they'd eat by the road in their car.

Once the gardener's wi turf drove past em
And my dad who was such a nut
Said, "thus what I'd do,
If I won a pound or two,
Send me lawn away ta be cut".

It was all these peculiar sayins
And their lovin as husband and wife
That made me real glad
Cos I know I had
The best Mum and Dad in my life.

COUNTRY LIFE

In the summer when out in the country
You smell the feint waft in the air
Of newly ploughed fields an ripe gardens
And the mountains of fresh laid manure.

You'll notice the farmers a workin
Harvestin crops for their yield
The cows will be out in the meadows
While the tractors are ploughin the fields.

My dad lorst his cap on a meadow
My heart he weren't half in a tis
He reckon he tried half a dozen on
Afore he found one that was his.

He worked the land for many years
An his mate at the time was Don
He reckoned he lorst his waistcoat
But dad said, "you're got ut on"

He was so glad he had found it
Cos theres no doubt about it
He say if you dint see I had that on
I woulda gone orf home wi'out it.

Another character on the farm
Who I can remember most
Was a chap called Billy North
Who was to meet Dad by a post.

"What if one of us is late?"
said dad to Billy North
"well if um there fust ull chalk a mark,
and if you're there fust, Rub it Orf".

I loved growin up in the country
In my younger days I'd climb trees
I'd go out n ma trousers were proper
But come home wi big holes in the knees.

My Dad he would make me a popgun
From elder and nuttery sticks
Then acorns were used as the bullets
And my heart we got up ta some tricks.

You never get bored in the country
There's so much to do and to see
I don't need bright lights and the City
My Country Life will do me.

HOME BAKING DAY

I remember the tempting aroma
Rock cakes layin hot on the tray
The currants all dark and like bullets
On Mothers home baking day.

I remember the hot sausage rolls
Laying out on a big metal griddle
Too hot, they'd come straight from the oven
My tongue burned when I bit in the middle.

Apple tarts well ya just wouldn't beat em
The pastry all floury and light
The apple was cut very finely
And melted when you took a bite.

Meat pies, cor! they made ya mouth water
All tasty, beefy and glazed
And a cup with a hole was inserted
To make sure the middle was raised.

The scraps of the pastry weren't wasted
Cos mother was eager to please
She would heat the dough balls in the oven
Take em out n then fill em wi cheese.

A diet? well it never was mentioned
And home cookin is so hard to beat
No rubbish or new fangled colours
Just good food that's a pleasure to eat.

THE OLD TIN BATH

Sunday night was bath night
The tub was made of tin
Such a treat
You couldn't beat
The feel when you got in.

By the fireside I sat bathing
My skin all young an dimples
One side of me
Red as can be
And the other side, "goose pimples".

Our bath was situated
By the fire set on the floor
The fire would glow
But the draught would blow
Under the kitchen door.

So one side of me was cosy
The other always cold
I couldn't turn
Cos the bath would burn
My bum…so I was told.

So I sat tight in ma water
And my little legs were pinned
And in times of troubles
My bath had bubbles
Made only by my wind.

We now have our home comforts
Where the bath is filled so free
No boiling pot
Cos the waters hot
It comes so easily.

I know I should be grateful
But it really was a laugh
The times I shared
With those who cared
By the fire in me Old Tin Bath.

THE FRONT ROOM

No one have em nowadays
Years ago they made a home
I hope you can remember
The outa bounds front room.

Used only just for Christmas
And for the party mood
When the big old drop-leaf table
Would be opened for your food.

Used only two or three times
For things throughout the year
All the best that people had
Was always kept in there.

All the smartest ornaments
Kept on the window sill
And fruit out on the table
When no one home was ill.

The three-piece suite not sat on
Except on special days
And the wallpaper of flock print
All gorn in different ways.

The open fire for comfort
Was lit before we woke
Because we hardly used it
It would fill the room wi smoke.

A little room of mystery
A little room of pride
Then they stuck you in your coffin
And laid ya in there when ya died.

THE PANTRY

Oh the fun in the pantry
A hoard of old n new
The tins and jars of marmalade
The stuff hid outa view.

I love ta search the corners
Where you find the odd cracked plate
And the big old bags a flour
A few months outa date.

You'll always find a lemon
All old n dark n bruised
Never to be thrown away
And you know that won't be used.

Jars of home made pickles
Wi bands around the top
Over tight bound greased proof paper
Lookin very near ta pop.

Two little dusty caddies
For ya coffees and ya teas
And I just now counted up
Eleven cans a garden peas.

The eight boxes of oxos
The powder tins for custard
Can't count how many pepper pots
and jars of Colmans Mustard.

And why do you find always
Inside the biscuit tin
A few old beaten packets
Wi just one hard biscuit in?

Theres most certainly a jelly
Bought wi good intention
Just cast aside, forgot about
Too many times ta mention.

Still with all the stuff that's lurkin
It would take forever more
To sort it out and tidy up...
So I shut the pantry door.

THE BUTTON TIN

It was once full of biscuits
They were a bingo win
It's now recycled into
A little button tin.

Be careful as you prod about
There's things you may not see
A badge pin that was stickin out
Once poked right into me.

As you delve amongst the unknown
Mind where you put your finger
Cos at the very bottom
There's many things that linger.

I like the little button cards
Wi different shapes and sets
And the cards wi shiny ringlets
That hold up curtain nets.

The old ones fascinate me
As sharp and hard as flint
And then theres them old tin ones
That always have a dint.

Always that big old brown one
The shade of rusty wire
All mis shaped and look as though
Thas been found in a fire.

Then five little yellow ones
From a set of six
With a tiny pattern on the front
Of little tiny chicks.

Badges from the Girl Guides
A photo of a car
And hooks and eyes on nylon
From the back of mothers bra.

A little silver sixpence
Now howd that get in there?
An a flower on a pinky clip
That went in someone's hair.

A button with an anchor
Not seen that before
And next time I look in the tin
I know I'll find some more.

OLD BOY ERNIE

He's a rummun is boy Ernie
But he's got a heart a gold
An allus sport a dew drop
On his nose wi out a cold.

His chequered hats lop-sided
His jacket's old n brown
His braces are pulled up ta stop
His pants a comun down

You'll see him in the summer
When the rest have shed their coats
The one still with his trousers
Tucked in his welly boots

He loves ta have a mardle
And most of who he meet
Hear tales of him and farm life
Top n tailin sugar beet.

He love ta do his garden
And trearpse round in the mud
You'll hear about his runner beans
And who've grown the biggest spud.

He has a tot a whisky
Each morn put in his tea
An he don't often ail much
Or so that seem ta be.

Now don't we love our Ernie?
And we all know him so well
A true old Norfolk gentleman
Wi the same old tales ta tell.

AUNTY LIL

Her car pull in the driveway
We all go quiet until
A gentle tap on the front door
"oh come in Aunty Lil".

Her stick like arms embrace you
Her lipstick rosy red
Embedded in your cheek until
thus time ta go ta bed.

The chants of,"bless her little heart"
En "blimey hint she grown"
Sometimes I felt like gorn outside
an bein on ma own.

The golden chains around her neck
Her laugh a squeaky pitch
The smell of perfume up ma nose
That made ma nostrils itch.

The big white leather handbag
Her hand go inside until
She bring me out a chocolate bar
"I love you Aunty Lil."

THE COUNTRY GARDEN

The coal bunker against the wall
A pail wi cinders in
The arch look good
All made of wood
Wi climbin plants stuck in.

The wood shed wi its yellow door
Holding logs sawn for the fire
And a wood pile lay
In a little bay
Near an old bike and a tyre.

The dog kennel, like a little house
A little bowl an dish
A lead that's gorn
Across the lawn
As far as you could wish.

A fresh vegetable garden
With a greenhouse by the side
A rabbits hutch
Not doin too much
Cos the poor old rabbits died

Oh I love my country garden
A little place of bliss
A place to wonder
Think and ponder
A place to reminisce.

MY GO-KART

My brother made a Go-kart
From dads old bits a wood
That went along a rummun
And that looked bloomun good.

The front wheels from a trolley
The rears were a pushchair
The bolts were from the garage
And the strings what made it steer.

I sat just on the rear wheels
Where he made a little seat
And either side the pivot bolt
Is where I put my feet.

I'd hold on ta the nylon string
To turn from left ta right
And get ready fa ma brother
I'd sit still n hold on tight.

He'd push me up n down the lane
As fast as he could go
He knew I was a tomboy
I dint like ta be pushed slow.

I loved ma little Go-Kart
But good things always end
I knew that when we crashed it
It was too broke up ta mend.

It ended very suddenly
I thought it was the pits
When I hit the bank at such a force
And the whole thing fell ta bits.

Somewhere on a scrapheap
Lay the toy that broke my heart
My one an only wooden car
My very own Go–Kart.

THE OUTSIDE TOILET

A little place to ponder
A place to sit n think
A brick built outside toilet
No comfort, heat, or sink.

The whitewashed walls inside
Were always cold n bare
Apart from huge great cobwebs
A hanging everywhere.

The seat that went across the pail
Was made of hardened wood
And cos we dint have any lights
That weren't always so good.

The paper on the roller
Was all we had to use
And if by Thursday that had gone
We'd use the Evening News.

I remember winter mornings
Traipsin snow beneath my feet
To get above that metal pail
On that cold old toilet seat.

So frightened by the darkness
The merest sound would make me freeze
And quite often I'd run out there
Wi me trousers round ma knees.

Cos today we have it always
In the comfort of our home
But I'll always have the memories
Of that dark cold murky dome.

OUR LITTLE ETHEL

Bless her little heart
Wi her pinny round her knees
She invite you in at any time
And share her cups a tea.

Her little hands all wrinkly
Her rings are all too big
Her hair is soft n curly
And look just like a wig.

All grey and neatly lacquered
Done by her home perm kit
But why always across the top
She hev that yellow bit?

A face of love and kindness
A world of work within
And lots a little tiny hairs
A pokin through her chin.

And lots of little fluffy balls
Hang round her cardi zipper
Her tights are dark an hanging
Quite loosely round her slipper.

The time I spend wi Ethel
She use to reminisce
I can't seem ta get a word in
So I just say no n yis.

She show me her new nik naks
And never do she fail
To say how much they cost her
At the local jumble sale.

Her little place is tidy
Not matching, but its clean
And a cactus planted in what was
A tub of Margarine.

That do me good ta visit
And I think without a doubt
The trouble wi this world today
There int enough like her about.

HOARDER TOMS OLD SHED

A hive of information
Of old and new and dead
Are found among the debris
Of Hoarder Toms old shed.

You traipse along the garden path
An eyesore you will see
But on opening the pitted door
That looked a gem ta me.

Old boxes up the corner
A bin, a fork, a hoe
And a rusty little mouse trap
Wi half a tail in tow.

And blast look at that cycle
The baskets old n brook
But thus worth a fair few bob ya know
If I aren't misunderstook.

An wus in that there box
I really want ta know
"cor blast me look at that,
thas an old Bush radio.

Shoved under the bench
I spy another box
Thus full a rusty nails n screws
And one of Mothers socks

Hey! Whats that paper covering
Over that tin pail ?
" blast there must be 90 beer mats,
that he bought from Acle Sale".

Theres a hammer wi no handle
Lawnmowers wi no blades
An suffin brown n smelly
On the bottom of the spades.

An old engine for a motorbike
On top that say a Norton,
He reckon that come from the bike
He rid about while courtin..

An afore I leave the 12 by 9
I turn around an stare
I could now go write Toms history
With what I found in there.

I LEARNT TA DRIVE A TRACTOR

Eight years old n feelin bored
Wi not a lot ta do
Dad said' gal you come alonga me
Ire gotta job fa you.

We walked to the allotment
And in the old Tin shed
Was Dads old Standard Fordson
And this is what he said,

"Ire gotta do some muck spreadun
N gal how would ya feel
If I went on the trailer,
N you behind the wheel"?

Well ma birthdays had come all at once
And ma Dad learnt me ta drive
Id been itchin ta do that
Since about the age of five.

He helped me back the tractor
N hitch the trailer on the back
Then we drove towards the muck heap
along the beaten track.

We loaded up n headed orf
And Dad wi two tine fork
Was on the trailer spreadin muck
And I was too amazed ta talk.

All of a sudden theres a forough
I thought ,"blast me this is it,
So I jammed the brakes on quickly
And ma dad fell in the….muck.

"Blast me gal what are ya dern?"
said dad so full of woe
but I had ta laugh cos all his clothes
were full a chicken poo.

So after all of this excitement
We both did have a laugh
And he stunk so much when we got home
Mum hulled im in the bath.

A LOOK INSIDE THE PUB

Oh! Ire gotta have a look
whatever do they do?
I feel quite inquisitive
cos I hint gotta clue.

Now, let me clean the window
and stand up on ma toes
ull look into the old pub room
showin just ma eyes and nose.

The men and women mardellin
their voices carry far
two men wi cards n matchsticks
on a little wooden bar.

Theres Brown Ale bottles everywhere
and not one can I reach
cos when I bring em down from home
I get a penny each.

The piano in the corner
a lady make her way
she open up the heavy lid
and really start to play.

Some people start a singing
the rest all clap and cheer
some on em don't do nothin
just sit and drink their beer.

Old Albert in the corner
forehead shiny as a pin
his braces pull his strides so high
they're right up ta his chin.

All cheerie happy people
behind the wooden door.
I hope the pubs are still like this
In 1984.

I climb down from the window
I've seen all I can see.
I hope my dad who's playin darts
Dint look up and see me.

A GOOD OLD JUMBLE SALE

Always on a Saturday
At the hall you'll never fail
Ta see the queue
At half past two
For the local Jumble sale.

Patiently awaitin
For bargains to explore
And for the day
You'll have ta pay
10 pence on the door.

As you enter, there's the kitchen
Cakes n teas lay out there ready
The happy looks
Of the local cooks
And a raffle for a Teddy.

The tables round the edges
They can cause quite a din,
Wi so much stuff
That can get rough
When they keep a pushin in.

There'll be Ethel wi her elbows
And you'll be lucky ta survive
When Molly Hoddy,
Wi her whole body,
Take a run and make a dive.

The shoes all laid out neatly
Near curtains, nets n coats
Where Val n Nova
Get scrappin over
Size 5 welly boots.

So give yourself a little treat
Because you'll never fail
To have fun and grab a bargain
At your local Jumble Sale.

A DAY OUT IN YARMOUTH

Have a day out in Yarmouth
A good time by the sea
Where sand is moist and plentiful
And at times the parkins free.

A walk along the golden mile
And have a bag a chips
Chance ya luck on the amusements
And on them there lucky dips.

Your'e gotta try the candy floss
Its on sale all the year.
Then go and see whats on
At night at Old Brittania Pier.

The good old indoor market
With plenty of choice stalls
You can buy most of the things you need
From knickers to footballs.

Don't you miss the bingo
Cos ive never missed it yet
The more tickets that you win and keep
The bigger prize you get.

Take a treck down Regent Street
With its shops and cafes and bars
And of course you've got the wax works
With its famous life like stars.

Now what about a game of bowls
Oh go on hire a lane
You really will enjoy yourself
And you'll keep dry if it rain.

If that fail theres the cinema
That's to name a few
So who don't go to Yarmouth
Cos theres nothin there to do ?

<u>THESE OLD BONES</u>

The same old bones
They share my world
The same old bones
All my fingers curled

The same old bones
In my legs as I dig
With a gap in the middle
I won't stop a pig.

With these old bones
Up and down to the bar
When I've drunk too much
They can't carry me far.

These old bones have seen things
That they shouldn't of seen
And been to some places
They shouldn't of been

My bones have held me
When I felt I would bend
My strength in my body
My bones my friend.